Depression

MOVING FROM DARKNESS TO *LIGHT*

WRITTEN BY EMMY KAVANAGH

PHOTOGRAPHS BY DAVID HEITUR

AuthorHouse™
1663 Liberty Drive
Bloomington, IN 47403
www.authorhouse.com
Phone: 1 (800) 839-8640

Published by AuthorHouse 10/03/2018

ISBN: 978-1-5462-5345-7 (sc)
ISBN: 978-1-5462-5465-2 (hc)
ISBN: 978-1-5462-5346-4 (e)

Library of Congress Control Number: 2018909021

Print information available on the last page.

authorHOUSE®

Dedication

This book is dedicated to the one soul that has touched mine deeper than any other. Mr. Raston, you brought joy and light into my life. During my darkness, you brought me strength and a reason to carry on. You will forever be my one and only soul mate. I miss you more than words can express and when you left this life, a piece of my heart went with you. My gentle giant, I will never forget you. I love you sir.

Introduction

Ever since I can remember I felt sad. I always felt like I was from another planet, less than, different from, not as smart as and always afraid of......everyone. Basically, comparing my insides to the rest of the world's outsides. I remember when I finally talked to my mom about my feelings of sadness, she completely understood. We came up with the analogy of one of those lead blankets, you know, the one that the dentist uses when he jams that uncomfortable contraption into your mouth for x-rays? I hate that thing, and it always makes me gag. I digress, anyway, it's like someone threw a giant lead blanket over my head and I had to walk around under that weight every day.

When I was a kid, I would always watch the birds and the butterflies and wish I could be them. I wished the breeze would take me away from everything and everybody, from myself, from the sadness and pain. My mind never stopped. All of the bad thoughts I had about myself would repeat themselves over and over again. As I got older, the feelings got worse. It was then that I found alcohol. When I took a sip of that beer, all of the chatter in my brain suddenly stopped. I had peace and quiet for the first time in my life. Alcohol became my best friend. I drank to escape the thoughts, the feelings, and the pain for a very long time. I know now, I was self-medicating.

I think I started going to therapy when I was around 22. It was hard for me to explain to someone how I felt. I didn't know why I felt this way, I just did. Nothing happened in my life to cause it, it just lived inside of me. It was so incredibly frustrating to not have a reason or something to point to and say, AH HA! That's it!! That's why I hate myself and want to die. No such luck.

Over time, the alcohol stopped working and all of those awful thoughts and feelings came back. The sadness was unbearable. Every therapist that I saw (and there were a lot of them), told me to quit drinking. I was trying to cure depression with a depressant and that doesn't work. But, I couldn't stop.

The Doctor's began to prescribe me medication. One pill after another and nothing worked. Sometimes I felt worse, sometimes I felt like a zombie, but never did I feel better. It got so bad, that I had to take a leave of absence from work. My best friend was so worried about me that he found my father's phone number and called him. He told my father that I was about to leave work and I was not in a good mental state. He told him that I owned a gun and he was worried about what I might do to myself. My father went to my house and removed the gun before I got there. My parents encouraged me to go into an outpatient mental health program which meant I would go to a facility every day from 9am until 2pm. It consisted of individual and group therapy, art therapy and cognitive therapy. I stayed in that program for several months. About a year after I went back to work, I had another breakdown and had to go out on another leave of absence and into the outpatient mental health program again. It would always help for a little while but, the feelings always returned. Usually worse than before. During both stints in that program, I had to stay with my parents. I owned my own home but was so crippled with depression and fear, I simply couldn't function or take care of myself.

After I returned back to my own home, it wasn't long before I spiraled into the deepest depression that I've ever had. I remember this one time I was laying on my couch. I had a bottle of whiskey, a beer and my gun all in front of me on the coffee table. I just kept staring at the gun, crying so hard with a terrible aching in the depth of my soul. My dog, Mr. Raston, was laying in the corner shivering. See, he was my soul mate. No human being can ever touch my heart and understand me like he did. I swear he had the soul of a wise old man and you could see it in his eyes. That is why I put the Mr. in front of Raston. He deserved the respect that you would give a wise old man. Anyway, I called out to him. At that very moment, he jumped up and walked over to me. He slowly climbed up on the couch, put his back paws on my toes and his head on my shoulder, stretching out across my entire body and let out a big sigh. He just lied there on top of me for what seemed to be hours, just holding me down. He knew that I was so close to ending it all. He saved my life that day. It was very soon after that that I decided to get some help with my drinking.

Through all of this I was still seeing professionals about my depression. When I quit drinking and found recovery, with the help of many angels, I thought I would finally feel better. That is what every therapist told me. I wish I could tell you that it worked but, it didn't. I had to go out on a leave of absence from work again and back into the outpatient program. I switched doctors yet again and became very frustrated when she suggested we change my medication….again. I was so tired of being a Guinea pig. It felt like with every doctor, every six months I was trying new medications and they never worked. This time though, it was different. Finally, something changed. This doctor found the right combination of medicine that finally made me feel like a normal person. I couldn't believe it, I no longer felt sad, lonely and hopeless. It was a miracle. I had never felt normal. Today, I am happy, joyous and free. I no longer feel the weight of darkness looming over me. I am free!

The purpose of this book is not to shock or upset anyone. It is not to make anyone feel guilty or hopeless. In fact, quite the opposite. The purpose of this book is to share my struggle. To bring awareness to the seriousness of mental illness and the critical need for more affordable programs and Doctors, help for those without health insurance, better facilities, and a deeper empathy for this disease. It is to give those who don't understand an inside perspective as to what this world looks and feels like through the eyes of someone who has experienced it. To bring hope to those who suffer and show them that they are not alone, that others suffer too. To bring hope that they too can overcome this disease and walk free.

If you know someone who is battling mental illness, please understand that there may not be enough love to take away all of their pain but, it can ease the suffering. So, tell them they are loved more often, hug them a little tighter, hold them when they cry and walk with them when they feel alone.

We are all human and if we just open our eyes, we can see that we all suffer in some way or another. If we just open our hearts, we can all feel the pain that our brothers and sisters feel. If we just pray, we can all come together and become one voice. Don't suffer in silence.

Darkness

This is the real me....

My mind is tired
Spinning around in circles
Around and around with no end in site
I just can't break the cycle
When someone speaks, I hear no words
It's like I don't care enough to retain their thoughts and feelings
My ability to focus on one thing at a time is impossible
I think and think and think....
What is wrong with me?
It's like I have checked out of life
No motivation or desires
I'm walking around in a fog that can't be lifted
I am oblivious
I can't think
I'm so clouded
I am lacking self confidence
I can't make decisions
The voices in my head are so loud....
You're stupid, ugly, unlovable, unlikable, unworthy of happiness, a waste of space
It NEVER ends
I hide some of these feelings because I feel like people will judge me
I lie even to you
I can't articulate where I am mentally
When I laugh, it is fake
I can't see the humor in anything
My smiles are empty
I have no energy

I can't keep up on any relationships
I can't hold a meaningful conversation
I'm empty
No words to speak
I feel like I have no personality
I don't know who I am
I never did
I'm so taken over by these awful, hurtful thoughts in my head
I don't know how to stop the tapes and replace them with positive thoughts
It feels like it is impossible
I'm so sad
I'm finally getting it out
This is the real me

My eyes scream for help but my voice remains trapped inside me

Minute by minute, link by link, I am bound by the chains of what is to become my prison

All the strength in my body cannot break the chains that imprison my soul

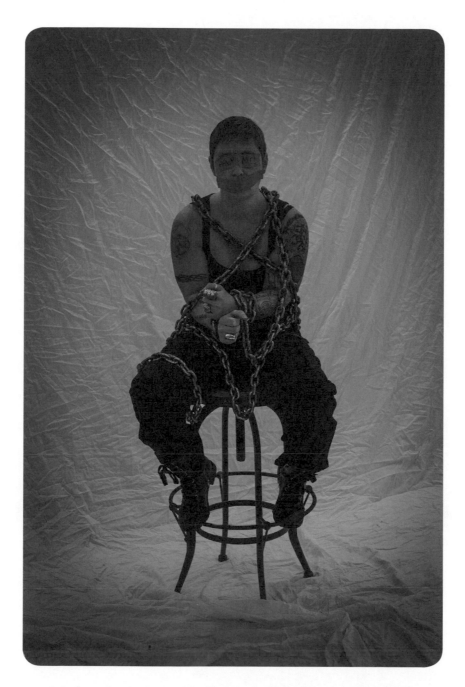

I lurk in the shadows of darkness, crippled with the feelings of self-hatred, despair and emptiness echoing through my soul….

Tortured Soul

I am so tired
Beaten
Tattered
Torn
My soul aches
My heart bleeds
Everything that I believed in is gone
I have wept over
I have begged for
I have craved for
Worth
Love
Devotion
I give those things
I give some more
In hopes to one day deserve the same in return
I wait
Why don't I deserve it?
I don't know
I wait
What have I done that is so bad that I should be punished?
I don't know
I wait
I want to be worthy
Please
I drop to my knees
I beg
I plead
Nothing....
Empty

Cold
Alone
Darkness
That is who I am
That is who I have always been
That is who I will always be
Is it true?
Recycled souls
Chosen paths
I did this???
I must hate myself more than I thought
All of my life
Since I remember
I have felt such a loneliness deep within
Why???
I am so tired
Tired of thinking
Tired of feeling
I give up
I give in
I've got nothing left to give
Why???
Nobody will give it back
Why???
I don't deserve it
Work
Fight
Stress
Beg
Cry

Plead
Nothing….
When does it end?
Never
Recycled souls
A continuation of punishment and solitude
I should find another damaged soul
Or maybe
Just maybe
I can find peace in something else
Something I can count on
Something that listens
Something that soothes me
Something that causes that burn
That pain
That good kind of pain
The kind that makes you feel worthy of it
The kind that helps you see in the darkness
That one little corner you never saw before
My core she says….
My core is a tortured soul
One that soars through the darkness like they are clouds
Do you know how I feel?
I think you do
I think you know exactly how I feel
Tortured soul
Tortured soul mate
You do don't you?
Sunshine and butterflies
They bring you peace

I think you feel rain clouds
Yea….
Rain clouds and vultures
Tortured soul
Tortured soul mate
Where are you?
Hiding?
Hiding in that deep, dark corner
I know baby
I can find you
Can you find me?

God....Where are you?

I don't know what is wrong with me
I don't know why I feel so sad all of the time
I don't know why I feel like I hold no value
I feel worthless and purposeless
I don't know why
Half of my feelings, I can't even articulate
I asked God to take me
How do I make this stop?
All of these thoughts of sadness, hate, anger and rage
I just want to go away
Far away from it all
I feel like nothing can make me happy
I just want to cry
My tears fall and burn my hands
They leave tracks on my cheeks
They leave marks on my soul
I just want it to go away
I feel so alone in this world of people
I'm sick of the violence
I'm sick of the ignorance
I'm sick of the prejudice
I'm sick of my heavy heart
God….why won't you help me
Why won't you lift these feelings from my mind, heart and soul?
Can't you stop these tears from falling?
Can't you dry my eyes?
Sometimes when I sit by the water
I see the beauty of your creations
I try to remember the good days, however few there are

But, I can't
My thoughts always return to all of the pain
My heart aches
My soul aches
My brain aches
I'm tired of the thoughts
I'm tired of the feelings
I'm tired of life
I listen to happy music….still sad
I listen to happy music….still enraged
I pretend I'm happy
I lie to everyone
I want to be happy
But happiness in others makes me angry
I just want it to stop
I want the voices to shut up
I want them to stop whispering poison into my thoughts
I want them to stop injecting poison into my body
I feel like it is flowing through my veins
Just waiting to kill me
Just take me before the poison sets in
Another holiday alone
They say I'm never alone
He is always present
Why can't I feel you?
Why won't you talk to me?
Can't you feel my pain?
Can't you hear my cries?
Can't you see my tears?
I try so hard to be strong but I feel so weak

I surrender to you and feel no change
I surrender to you and see no results
I just want peace
If you are the almighty Savior
If you are the one that has all power
If you are the one that has all love
Where is it?
Make all of the pain go away
Make it stop
Love me
Lift me up
Fill me with your love and peace
I'm begging you….
HELP
I'm begging you….
Let me love myself
I'm begging you….
Let me see the light
Help me through the tunnel and over the hill
Let me see the peace on the other side
Let me see the light on the other side
Let me feel you on the other side
Let me feel grace, beauty and love
Let me be free
Please, just let me be free

The Water

When will the hurting stop
I feel like I am burning alive under my flesh, in my
heart and soul
The flames are so big, so hot and so fierce
Even the ocean can't extinguish them
The light from the flames glow through my eyes like
embers through the air
No one sees them
They must be invisible, like me
Someone call the fire department
Someone throw a glass of water on it
Someone smother it
Someone do something
Anything to stop the burning pain inside me
Do you think someone can fill these holes in my heart
with purpose, love and hope?
I don't
I am all alone in this world of pain, self-hatred and
sadness
I am all alone to sit in my anger and rage
Sometimes, I wish it would end
Sometimes I wish I could end it myself
Sometimes I wish I would never wake up
Beauty and Grace never seem to find me
They lurk in the shadows of the unreachable happiness
The burdens and weight upon my back are unbearable
The heaviness in my heart is too much for me to carry
The willingness to fight for happiness and peace is slowly
floating away with the waves
Maybe I should float away with the waves

Maybe the sea will fill my lungs with salt water
My lungs will begin to fill with the very ocean that can't
extinguish my flames
Don't drink the water they say
I have to
How else will I end the pain?
How else will I end this loneliness?
Please Emmy….
Drink the water

Alone

Alone again
No wife to have
Alone again
No love to give
Alone again
Heart shattered
Alone again
No arms around me
Alone again
No one to tell me it's ok
Alone again
More voices in my head
Alone again
No way to quiet them down
Alone again
Who gives a fuck
Alone again
Suffer in silence
Alone again
Feel the pain
Alone again
Not worthy of love
Alone again
Yup, alone again
As usual
Alone again
What the fuck do you expect!

*Every nerve in my body is exposed. When a gentle breeze blows, some feel
relief, I feel a burning pain radiating through my soul….*

L;GHT

There is hope....you can conquer the beast.

A new Journey

There is something about water that brings me peace
It's one of the few things that looks beautiful all of the time
At night, the way the moon dances across the peaceful, calm bay
It takes my breath away
On a hot, sunny day
The way the sun glistens against the rough ocean waves
It gives me the overwhelming need for a long peaceful exhale
One that cleanses your soul
On that warm spring day
When it just begins to sprinkle
The raindrops bounce around the shiny pond water
It brings this smile across my face
One that is contagious
And my favorite
On that chilly, fall day
When I walk along that cute, rocky creek
Weaving through the woods
Orange and yellow leaves drop from the trees
They float along on their new journey
I want a new journey
One filled with laughter
Smiles
Passion
Safety
Love
Peace
I'm tired of where I have been

Darkness
Sadness
Worthlessness
Pain
I don't want that anymore
I don't know any different
I don't know happy
And I certainly don't know how to get there
I don't think it will be easy
I don't think it will always be fun
I don't think the road will be smooth
Or straight for that matter
I don't think it will be a quick journey
But it's one that I want to take
Yes….
A new journey

May love and light rain down upon you as soft and gentle as petals from a beautiful flower

My Hope for You

I know all you see is darkness
I know all your heart feels is loneliness
I know all your soul feels is emptiness
I know all you hear is the echo of your silent screams
I know you feel like there is no end to these feelings
That life isn't worth living
That nobody cares
That nobody will miss you
That all you will see is grey for the rest of your life
Please….
DON'T GIVE UP
There is light in this world
You will feel whole again
You will feel happy again
People love you
You will see in color again
Stay strong
You are beautiful
Walk with your head held high
Tell someone your struggle
Open your heart just a little bit
Trust in someone
Let them hug you
Let them love you
Know that there is someone in this world
Who is struggling like you
Know that there is someone in this world
That knows your pain
I know your pain
The struggle was real for me

It was painful
I felt all of those feelings that you do now
But….
I asked for help and found it
It took a long time to get it right
It took a long time to work through the changes
But it worked
I smile today
I hear birds singing
I smell flowers
I see butterflies
Fighting through all of the pain
All of the darkness
All of the loneliness
All of the emptiness
Was worth the peace I feel now
You are worth fighting for
You are loved
Please have faith
A Power greater than you is present
That Power will help you get through this
That Power will give you the strength
To overcome your battle
You will conquer this
Please….
Stay strong
This is my hope for you

There is beauty in life

After the Darkness

My soul feels whole again
My heart feels complete
My head is quiet
I am at peace
I smile
I laugh
I love deeply
I speak clearly
I see beauty
I hear music
I feel content
I wake up grateful
I sleep soundly
I hug tighter
I embrace life
I embrace joy
I finally feel the warmth
I finally see the light
My life is beautiful
This is what lies....
After the darkness

Like the roots of a tree, my strength continues to grow.

I can now see the beauty in my life and everything around me

My Savior

With the wind at my back, I shall escape my resistance
With the sun warming my face, I shall feel no chills
I can use the rays of your light to illuminate my path
With your guidance, I will persevere
With your love, I will overcome adversity
Your creations make life beautiful, I will care for them
Your comfort can bring me peace
With your understanding, I can be a better woman
With your grace, I can love again
With your almighty power, I can forgive
I am standing tall in your presence
I can feel your touch embrace me
I know you are in my heart and a part of my soul
I will turn my will and life over to your care
My Almighty, with your patience, I will embrace life again
I will feel the love, joy and sadness that life brings
I know you will walk with me through life's journey
I am your child
I can now feel your love
Thy will, not mine, be done!

Dave – I am amazed at your ability to put yourself into the thoughts and feelings of someone else in order to capture the purpose and emotion of the moment. You sir, are a genius. I could not have accomplished this without your brilliance!

It takes a village….

Mom and Dad, your hugs, kisses and the fact that you were always there to pick up the pieces got me through it. I love you both with all of my heart and I appreciate all of your love and support. Thank you Shelly, Tommy, Punkin', Chris and Ashley for your unconditional love. Ken, you literally saved my life. I can never express my gratitude and love for you. Dave, your love, support and protection was always just what I needed. Mike and Glenn, your encouragement to do what was best for myself and get the help that I so desperately needed means the world to me. Joann, Lynn and Dalton, you all listened and supported me every step of the way. Deena, my BFF, you were my rock. You were the one that stood by me and always understood my challenges. You always spoke with wisdom and love. You propped me up sis. I'll never forget it. Kathryn, you were gentle and kind when I needed it the most. Tracie, what can I say, you supported me from the beginning to end. You are my oldest and dearest friend and I love you. Liz, you always loved me no matter what. Angie, you always understood like nobody else. Amia, during our time together, you so gently held my hand through it. Chrissy, you always appeared at just the right time. Lester and Pam, thank you for encouraging me to share this with the world. To all my sisters and brothers in the rooms, you will all live forever in my heart. You guys loved me until I could love myself. To all of those that I missed, thank you. Above all, I am alive today because my Higher Power put all of you in my life. We are all His children, and He loves us all.

Printed in the United States
By Bookmasters